PRAISE FOR LC

WORDS LIKE THUNDER:
NEW AND USED ANISHINAABE PRAYERS

"With a text richly packed with facts, tales, and voices we all need to know more about, Beardslee slices through categorizations and refreshes truth."

—Naomi Shihab Nye, *New York Times Magazine*

"Reflective, inspiring, thought-provoking, deftly written."

—*Midwest Book Review*

"The Abenaki poet and storyteller Joseph Bruchac would frequently end his letters with the phrase, 'Walk in Balance.' *Words like Thunder* is a vivid recipe for application of that wish in the present day."

—*Rain Taxi*

"'Our literature is a thin film that wraps itself around us,' writes Beardslee. For all their fragility, these story poems are cause for celebration. They paint a picture of contemporary Anishinaabe life as vivid as the wild berries she conjures for us."

—Armand Garnet Ruffo, author of *Norval Morrisseau: Man Changing into Thunderbird*

"Beardslee's 'new and used Anishinaabe prayers' are a rich combination of prose poetry, storytelling, and delights born both of the earth and the ether."

—*Petoskey News-Review*

"Beardslee is back with artful prayers in the form of poignant story and poem. Like her own birch bark art, she has chiseled with tooth and nail a human experience in the US that claims more than a moment in history. *Words like Thunder* defines Lois Beardslee's literary prowess indefinitely."

—Sheila A. Rocha, chair of performing arts at
the Institute of American Indian Arts

WE

LIVE

HERE

MADE IN MICHIGAN WRITERS SERIES

general editors

Michael Delp, Interlochen Center for the Arts
M. L. Liebler, Wayne State University

A complete listing of the books in this series can
be found online at wsupress.wayne.edu.

WE LIVE HERE

poems for an
ojibwe
calendar year

Lois Beardslee

Foreword by Molly McGlennen

Wayne State University Press
Detroit

ISBN 9780814351468 (paperback)
ISBN 9780814351475 (e-book)

Library of Congress Control Number: 2024931669

Cover and interior illustrations by Lois Beardslee.
Cover and interior design by Lindsey Cleworth.

Publication of this book was made possible by a generous gift from The Meijer Foundation.

Wayne State University Press rests on Waawiyaataanong, also referred to as Detroit, the ancestral and contemporary homeland of the Three Fires Confederacy. These sovereign lands were granted by the Ojibwe, Odawa, Potawatomi, and Wyandot Nations, in 1807, through the Treaty of Detroit. Wayne State University Press affirms Indigenous sovereignty and honors all tribes with a connection to Detroit. With our Native neighbors, the press works to advance educational equity and promote a better future for the earth and all people.

Wayne State University Press
Leonard N. Simons Building
4809 Woodward Avenue
Detroit, Michigan 48201–1309

Visit us online at wsupress.wayne.edu.

CONTENTS

FOREWORD

"Our stories are our lives," writes Lois Beardslee. Shaped and delivered through poetry, the stories Beardslee tells in her important collection, *We Live Here*, gently carry and keep Ojibwe history and lifeways. For me, this is one of the most resonant and distinct qualities of poetry: to creatively index that which is closest to our hearts.

I love collections that have an organizational hook, and Beardslee's certainly delivers this as she designs a poetic framework around an "Ojibwe calendar year," revealing the potency of the Anishinaabe language and cultural practices. Beardslee explains to her reader that "Traditional Anishinaabe ways of accurately storing and teaching information have always been specialized in regard to time and place, so our calendar system has historically been specific to different locations and microclimates throughout the Great Lakes." In this way, poetry becomes the teacher in this collection. It is a compass and an archive at once, and because of this, Beardslee adopts poetry not as an object or container but as the reader's animate guide *on the move*. When we read Beardslee's poems, we feel accompanied and cared for.

Perhaps one of the things I admire most about *We Live Here* is that it operates almost entirely from an Anishinaabe worldview. In addition to using Ojibwe language throughout, the collection remains indefatigably attentive to the organizations of Anishinaabe life cycles. This allows Beardslee a creatively Indigenous structure that communicates the cultural signposts of Anishinaabe knowledges and their relevance and relationship to contemporary Ojibwe people. This unique organization, moreover, illuminates the shortcomings of settler-colonial, capitalist approaches to foster a healthy planet. Extractive methods run counter to the relational methods on which Beardslee's poems run.

In Beardslee's collection, poetry is an expression of relationality. For starters, the word "for" in her subtitle explicitly marks the entire collection as an act of dedication. And as an act of dedication, the collection has a strong sense of its reader/listener, with some of the best poems vibrating with Indigenous land knowledge, such as "Namebinigiizis" and "Miinikewigiizis." In fact, most of the poems read like cultural annals and forecasts informed by Ojibwemowin, indicating the depth and vibrancy a Native language holds and carries. Like many Indigenous poets writing today, Beardslee suggests that poetry is one way in which Native knowledges can be ethically collected and disseminated for future generations.

In the beautifully lyrical "Namebinigiizis," Beardslee writes "Listen. / Shhh . . . / I want to talk to you about the sounds that the ice makes." The speaker goes on in the poem to relay the wisdom of the suckerfish as the "Suckers know more than men about the change of seasons," and are the ones that can tell all animate beings who might be listening when the ice will begin to break up off the lakes. Not only do the suckers augur a sort of almanac, but they also tell a cautionary story: mind the ice or you could fall through. "Suckers know about spring, even when it's far away," Beardslee writes, reminding her reader that wisdom-keepers are also non-human, that all beings have forms of communication. Lyricism can be a way to transliterate the sounds and messages around us humans.

There is a long line of Anishinaabe storytellers who use poetry, memoir, and fiction *on the move*. One of the progenitors of this style is Ignatia Broker and her Ojibwe narrative *Night Flying Woman*. In some ways I read Beardslee's collection as a direct literary descendant of that text for the way they each attend to Ojibwe language and culture "based on oral tradition" and its "importance of memory, listening, and speaking" (Broker 1983, ix). Broker's narrative tells the story of her great-great-grandmother, Oona, living through a period of immense disruption and loss for the People. Despite this, Broker's story stresses continuance through the adherence to core Ojibwe values, one of which is paying attention: "Little Oona awoke on bright new day to the busy stirrings of the village. . . . 'Bis-in-d-an, listen,' Oona whispered to herself, heeding one of her first lessons. 'Listen, and you will hear the patterns of life'" (1983, 21).

In that same tradition, Beardslee's attention to Ojibwe-specific values emphasizes how those concepts live in the Anishinaabe language. Her poems, like the language itself, act as storehouses of knowledge and show what holds fast when a poet fuses tribally specific knowledge into verse. Another incredible Ojibwe poet, Kimberly Blaeser, has stressed the importance of "Indigenizing contemporary poetry by writing in traditional languages." As founding member of the organization Indigenous Nations Poets (In-Na-Po), Blaeser initiated the #LanguageBack program that "centers poetry's role in language revitalization." In-Na-Po's "Language Back" webpage explains, "Poetry in Indigenous Languages can become a vehicle for expanding access to Traditional Knowledge and cultural practices within tribal communities, and sharing those teachings in service of climate change intervention." *We Live Here* heeds this call entirely.

As much as Beardslee's work is engaging and stretching these larger considerations taken up by poetry, her poems also thrive in their everydayness. Indeed, the vernacular signals profundity in the world of the poems, in the way "The kids want to know why Nanaboozho poked his finger into the bark on the maple sugar tree," and in the way "he slept sitting up / In front of the fire / . . . While whitefish / Danced over the coals / On long greenwood planks." *We Live Here*'s resonance lies in its structure and texture. At her very multimodal best, Beardslee weaves her own artwork throughout the collection, bringing visuality to the storytelling around the Ojibwe calendar—the everydayness. A distinguished visual artist, Beardslee braids her illustrations with the poems reflecting the fluid, watery movement of Anishinaabeg beings, lands, and stories. Acting as interludes, the visual works act as resting places along the living pathways Beardslee's reader is following.

Like a good storyteller, Beardslee meets the needs of her listener. *We Live Here* teaches as it depicts the complexities and beauty of Ojibwe culture—the "uninterrupted cultural ties" are learned "through daily practical events," she reminds us. In this way, "traditions" are not revealed as incongruous with modernity but rather as essential to Indigenous futures on behalf of Native peoples' progeny, cultural patrimony, and homelands.

As a reader of Beardslee's poems, I feel gratitude—gratitude for the gift of creative spirit that delivers a uniquely essential part of Anishinaabe intellectual traditions. And as you step into the collection, I trust you, too, will "put your ear to the ice," listen, and feel reassured that you will have your bearings, your direction, toward that softening horizon.

Molly McGlennen

WORKS CITED

Broker, Ignatia. *Night Flying Woman: An Ojibway Narrative.* St. Paul: Minnesota Historical Society Press, 1983.

INTRODUCTION

I enjoy being a modern Anishinaabe person with strong cultural traditions, blending the old with the new. The Anishinaabeg (Ojibwe a.k.a. Chippewa) are an Indigenous people who've lived on and around the Great Lakes for thousands of years, and we're still living here today, straddling what has become a modern international border. I feel lucky because my family has always been here. Adaptation and modernity are strong traditional values for us. I do not consider traditional ideas or activities to have been frozen in time or place. I live in a modern world, but I've also been able to live, work, and raise my children in remote places where uninterrupted cultural ties to the environment have been fairly easy to learn through daily practical events. My writing often reflects a blend of ancient and modern that I take for granted as part of an Anishinaabe worldview.

Some of my poems are funny, some are serious, and some just reflect things I've seen, done, felt, or maybe just worried about. Some are written in my own voice, and some are written in the voices of my children, my elders, or other friends and family members. I like doing that because it reminds me that a lot of life's experiences are shared by other people. Sometimes people's adventures get whittled down through time and become stories that turn into a kind of cultural shorthand for teaching important information, not just about the environment, but about getting through life on a daily basis. Cultural outsiders may refer to such cultural contractions as myths or legends, but to us, they are history. They may refer to the characters in our stories as spirits, but to us, they are family. Our stories are our lives.

In this collection, I chose to organize poems around a traditional Anishinaabe annual calendar, to emphasize the circular and practical natures of our traditions and their dependence upon the landscape in which they developed over a long period of time. The calendar gave me a framework for writing about what it's like being an Anishinaabe person living in two cultures on a day-to-day basis, sometimes happy and sometimes serious, sometimes just playing with stories and language. Cultures mingle, bend, break, mend, and change when different people encounter one another, so contemporary Anishinaabe families have learned to live with both traditional and modern ways of organizing information. Events like wild rice harvests don't happen at exactly the same time every year. Wild rice might ripen in either August or September according to the Roman calendar; but it can only ripen during the Ricing Moon in the Ojibwe calendar. Today, things like the Roman calendar and base ten number systems are used in North American schools by everyone, but they have a relatively short history in Anishinaabe territory.

The territory of the Anishinaabe people covers thousands

of square miles surrounding the northern Great Lakes in parts of what are now known as the United States and Canada. It is so large that it contains many different microclimates. So, traditional names for our months can vary from one community to another. Plants, animals, ice, and other environmental phenomena respond differently to events like spring warming in our southern regions than in the northern areas. These changes even vary with elevation or proximity to large bodies of water. At any given time, Anishinaabe people in one place might find the spring harvest of fish as memorable, while relatives in a different place might remember personal events related to damage caused by heavy, wet spring snows. During some years, the Sucker Moon, when large schools of fish break up thin ice while going upriver to spawn, might happen as early as the Roman calendar month of March. Other years it might not happen until as late as May, even in the exact same location. Because of this variability, the concept of the month of March might translate into Anishinaabemowin, the Ojibwe language, as Sucker Moon one year and as Breaking Snowshoe Moon the next year; or both names might be used any given year but in different communities.

The Anishinaabe month system isn't so much a calendar as a system of organizing historic information for practical purposes, like planning ahead to organize work or travel schedules. Traditional Anishinaabe ways of accurately storing and teaching information have always been specialized in regard to time and place, so our calendar system historically has been specific to different locations and microclimates throughout the Great Lakes. In a Roman calendar, months are not all the same number of days in length, so the visible crescent of a new moon begins on a different day every month. In an Anishinaabe calendar, the visible crescent of a new moon begins on the first day of every month. It takes the moon twenty-eight days to go through its cycle of increasing and diminishing visibility in the night sky, so each Anishinaabe "month" is twenty-eight days long and is labeled in our language as a "moon." That adds up to thirteen months, with names based upon observations of biological and geological events and how we humans interact with them. It is an accurate system of recording and predicting when things are likely to happen in an environment, but it is also very fluid.

Weather varies from year to year, so by naming months or "moons" after events and activities, Anishinaabe people have been able to remember and record things as they really happened to us, without being tied to a rigid numerical calendar that doesn't reflect actual lived experiences. Because this flexible system has always concentrated on important environmental and cultural events, it allows today's Anishinaabeg to accommodate two states of mind: contemporary and traditional. The Anishinaabe moon-based calendar system wasn't designed for things like planning an appointment at a dentist's office, but it serves its purpose, and it deserves our respect.

As our world changes, from moon to moon, from year to year, and from generation to generation, modern Anishinaabe people remain fully aware of our cultural traditions, adjusting how we use them among ourselves and to interact with others. We are a modern people who live side by side with people from other cultures. We've learned to adapt how we present ourselves, our histories, and even time itself, to interact with and teach others. We have several different traditional Anishinaabe month names that we can use to refer to each of the twelve contemporary Roman calendar months. To reconcile the Roman calendar with our own thirteen-moon system, I've chosen to use the name Ricing Moon twice, both at the beginning and the end of this poetry cycle. This moon occurs in late summer or early fall, a time of year that corresponds with intensive food harvesting for winter storage in a northern environment. A time of transition in terms of our schedules of ceremony, work, and play, historically the Ricing Moon has been the beginning and end of each Anishinaabe year. This reflects the cyclical nature of our reckoning of time and place in the world. We are modern people with an ancient, flexible culture. We have been here forever. We live among you today. We will be here for a long time, no matter which calendar we use to organize our lives or where we choose to use it.

Manoominikegiizis

RICING MOON

Morning, before the wind was up
Before the angriest of her relations shook the skies
She moved in gentleness
Lit the first candle of the day
Coaxed the stove into crackles and heat
Sipped strong, hot teas.
   Mashkiiigobag
      Bagoooosan
         Waabooswawaaaaskwanminan
           Papashkikiu.

She stole time, before the wind was up
Before the neediest of her relations shook the household
She moved in gentleness
Slid out onto the lake
Stirred the rails and the shiibshiibshiibducks into
   consciousness
Stole silent glances from restless life forms.
   From grazing ruminants
      Huuungry snakes
         Spiiiraling preeedators
           Mindful prey.

She created love, before the wind was up
Before the most jealous of her lovers shook her presence of
   mind
She moved in gentleness
Reached out for long, supple stalks
Held the body of that rice to her own
   Felt the give and take of the stems
      The strength of the husks
         The firmness of the berries
            The coolness of morning's moisture.

Morning, before the wind was up
Before responsibilities and foolishness wooed her away
She moved in gentleness
Planning ahead for the next liaison
Joining together in a marriage of convenience the most
   mature of those wiiild rice stalks.
   Some for the ducks
      For wooorms and snails and buuugs
         For the faaamily.
            The rest for the bottom of the lake.

Minowichige

RESPONSIBILITY

Everyone expects
    her to do it
Relies upon
    her love for the task
Outsiders might
    give her a title
Call it
    her job
But she loves
    watching the rice
She never wastes
    a single grain

She caresses
    the seed heads
She pinches
    the seed heads
She bundles
    the seed heads
She sings about
    the seed heads
She dreams about
    the seed heads
She teaches about
    the seed heads

She loves
    the seed heads

Some for the ducks
    For wooorms and snails and buuugs
    For the faaamily.
        The rest for the bottom of the lake.

Manoomin

WILD RICE

I don't remember, don't remember when my mother showed me the rice. Must have been a very little girl when my mother showed me the rice. Because I've almost forgotten that I was a little girl and I knew about that rice.

Didn't care about the muck or the leeches or the things that poke the soft part of your foot or the squish, squish, squish between your toes. Just wanted to please my mother, show her I know how to learn from that rice.

Maybe that rice is ready now. And I walk up the road past modern plantation pines, past where we catch turtles from an underwater sand point. Past straight-edged property lines. Past jagged electrical lines. I want them, I want them, I want them someday to come to my house. I'm off to remember that rice. . . . My mother's rice.

Rice in my palms, rice in my pockets, rice in the folds of my shirts. She'll take any bits of ripe sweet rice I bring her. Just a taste. A taste of before the electrical lines that I want, I want, I want someday to come to my house. She says that we used to live over there when she was a little girl, before the electrical lines, where they used to harvest that rice.

I don't remember, don't remember when my grandmother stole off in early morning canoes and showed my mother the rice. Must have been a very little girl when her mother showed her the rice. Because she'd almost forgotten that she was once a little girl and she knew about that rice, before the electrical lines.

I show my girl, I show my girl, show my girl how to remember that rice. We sneak along past modern plantation pines, where I used to catch turtles from an underwater sand point. Past straight-edged property lines. Past jagged electrical lines. They never, they never, they never came to my house. I show her how to find that rice. . . . My grandmothers' rice.

So, show your daughters, show your daughters where to live with that rice. Don't care about the muck or the leeches or the things that poke the soft part of your foot. Don't care about straight-edged property lines. Don't care about jagged electrical lines. Show them not to forget that you were a little girl and you know about that rice. . . . Your daughters' rice.

Gidanimibiisaa na

LET'S PADDLE AWAY

Let's paddle away
to the few places left
where pike have not been poisoned
by electrical transformers,
away from view-lot subdivisions
that squeeze out people like me
who only know how to paddle harder and harder
into mercurial winds
that do not acknowledge their own lack
of geologic history.

Let's portage away
to crevices that do not embrace
outboard motor–driven consumption
of the last loon-nest islands
or squeeze out people like me
from stressful proximity
to vulnerable waterfowl.

Let's paddle away
to a place where
my memories can survive.

Waatebagaagiizis

CHANGING COLOR MOON

It is with
the utmost sincerity
that I apologize
for the disruption.

I realize
that our presence here
interfered with
your enjoyment
of our front yard.

And the boy,
the boy, he was just curious,
not having seen your kind
close-up.

So, I apologize
for our presence
in this place
that you have
staked out as your own.

And this is the time of year
that you usually use this particular spot
to rest,
to recreate.

You see,
it has been many generations
since my family
owned land
on a south-facing slope.

So, we have no one
to turn to
for social skills
on this particular issue.

Your etiquette
and mine
do not necessarily match,
do not necessarily congeal
or result in something as convenient as a cultural colloid suspension,

Because you are a snake
and your whole family is made up
of snakes—
garter snakes, to be exact . . .

And now,
now that warm, sunny slopes
and south-facing beaches
are rare commodities
in Ojibwe country,
we are at odds over resources.

Ginebigoog

SNAKES

That was a difficult conversation
The one that Ninooko had with the snake.
"Waatebagaagiizis aawi."
Snake unhinged her jaw
To gulp down the sunshine between Noko's toes.
Days getting shorter.
Trees saying goodbye to summer.
The patch of sunshine on this north slope
Is now so small
That mother snake is forced
To converse with Indian women
And small Indian boys
Who are more than willing
To share the brief warmth
Of autumn spiraling
Into winter's sleep.
Ginebig asked Ninooko
Which one of us is going to survive
Here
Absorbing the dwindling resource.
And the old lady told the snake
It's OK.
We're both
Going to make it.
And for a little while
I thought she was talking to me.

Namegosag

TROUT

Funny
How
Everybody thinks
The fish
From
Their own lakes
Taste better
Than
Everybody else's.

Funny
How
We rely
Upon
Their predictability
To put away
Food
For winter's
Short, dark workdays.

Funny
How
My hands

Feel smooth
From fish fat
Like
A Navajo or a Hopi
Butchering a sheep.

Minaniki

BERRY PICKING

Time
was not always generous to my mother
who said that she worked more hours for less pay
than people who did not necessarily need the fruit
to nurture either their bodies or their souls.

Some years
she took us to pick blueberries in red-leaved fields
after they had been kissed by frost and plants hurried to
    finish their missions;
she took us to pick cranberries
after there was ice in the bogs and grouse had had their fill.

Some seasons
she watched over her shoulder and side-stepped fresh stools
all the while singing of friendly bears and warm autumn
    afternoons,
never letting us wander more than an arm's length from her
    intuition,
imagining on the back of her own neck a fat bear's hot
    breath.

Gashkadinogiizis

ICE-FORMING MOON

Goldfinch
Almost domesticated
Store-bought
Seed-fed
Golden shining bird.

Blown
Off course
By blood-deep
Intuition,
Endangered individual.

Clinging
To familiar
Windowpanes
In unfamiliar
Northern climes.

Looking
Hoping
Needing
Surplus
In Indian Country.

Manisaanabe
Miigaadi Biboon

FIREWOOD MAN VS. WINTER

He can't stop
Working.

He thinks that maybe one more log can be pulled out of
    those woods
lifted from beneath the snow
cut up to manageability
moved down a beach
hauled up a path
split
stacked
dried
coveted
relied upon
savored
respected
enjoyed
inhaled like perfume.

He can't stop
Working.

He thinks that maybe one more heavy, wet blanket can be
    pulled down from his camp in the north
to force rest and quiet and sleep upon
windblown hillsides
desiccated leaves
aggressive saplings
fruit-swollen heathers
soft mosses
pollinating midges
hesitant moths
mud-burrowed crayfish
ancient turtles
earthbound snakes
fattened squirrels
pregnant bears
industrious men.

Bagaanag

PLENTY

She can tell you exactly when the stems on the wild nuts
    were loosened from the trees
By ancient distant relatives, like Biboon, whose sole purpose
    in life
Was to provide for her and her family endlessly in a cascade
    of generations
Falling one upon the other in a history as vast as the
    continent itself.

She will sit across from you at her small table
And she will finger each of the nuts loosely in an open bowl
As though passing life itself onto each of the bristly husks
Before passing them to you as gifts of joy and sustenance in a
    tradition as fluid as time itself.

Her fingers have always coaxed outer husks from those
    shells before the task becomes dry and difficult
Maximizing every movement and opportunity to store away
    the preceding months of fat and plenty
Putting away sweets and fruits and seeds heady with the
    fragrance of growth and summer's solstice and oil-based
    stores of sunshine
With meats and fishes and pollens and leaves and flours and
    tubers.

She can tell you exactly when she tripped through the close
    firs and birch
In search of fungus pushed up like her mother's fingers
    prodding her from relaxation and slumber,
Like a steady-handed parent coaxing each growing season
    into adolescence and the acquisition of survival
By learning to love one's resources, to celebrate one's
    resources, to dance around one's resources, to fondle and
    imbue with forever one's resources.

Waawaashkeshikwe

VENISON

Of all of the Antlered Ones I have consumed
the one that stays in my memory
was from the only time, only time ever

That my father's shot did not fly true,
and when we followed him smiling
to retrieve our future sustenance,

Waawaashkeshikwe looked at us in terror
and tried to raise her numbed hindquarters
while he cried out loud and put a bullet through her
    forehead.

And my mother prayed out loud through her tears
in Ojibwe words I did not know she remembered
or had time and inclination to share with me.

Back at our barn she rinsed out the liver,
tried to wash panic-filled blood from lungs and heart,
pushed hand-whittled tobaccos onto a frothed tongue.

The next day we tried to eat the heart,
as we do every autumn,
but the meat was too thick with self-deception.

And all that winter
she taught me old prayers
that she never before thought I might need.

Manidoogiizans

DECEMBER

When I asked my mother
If she could remember
What her mother's mother called December
Before the Black-Robed religious reformers
Named it LittleSpiritMoon
After their BabyJesus

She put her open hand
To her own lips
Shook her head
Looked away
Said we are better off
If we do not remember those things.

Gabo Wendaamowin

LAKE SUPERIOR OJIBWE GOSSIP SONG

The more we get together, together, together...
We sat all together, stiffly, on metal folding chairs, in one
stained glass room,
In that institution they called the boarding school.
A nun came once a week to play four chords on her guitar,
and she sang to us.

Ooh waah, ooh waah, oo-ooh waa-ah, ooh waah...
We wanted it to be Frankie Lyman and the Teenagers.

The more we get together, together, together...
We weren't allowed to talk to each other, because it would
make us cry for one another.
We especially could not converse in what was left of our
Ojibwe.
Maybe the nuns thought we were gossiping about ... them.

The more we get together, the happier we'll feel...
My older sister rolled her eyes at me.
She motioned to Sister, made a sign for the bathroom, then
slid down the empty hallway.
I waited, then did the same, escaping into silence.

The more we get together, together, together . . .
My sister came out of the bathroom crying.
She kicked the wall, hugged me,
Then punched me, not too hard.

Ooh waah, ooh waah . . .
"Are you having *achiiside*?" I whispered.
She winced up behind me, at the approaching nun.
"Yeah, I'm having a *cheesy* day."

Oo-ooh waa-ah, ooh waah . . .
We had to put our sleeping mats on opposite ends of the
     hallway floor,
Silent girls in silent rows,
Too many of us for the allocated beds,
My sister and I a mile apart.

The more we get together, together, together . . .
Years later, in college dormitories, I kept early lessons close
     to my heart . . .
Nights, listening to cars drive by, I pretended the sounds of
     wheels on pavement
Were really waves on the beach at my family's noisy little
     house.

Ooh waah, ooh waah . . .
Oo-ooh waa—pagaask waashkaa.

Dibikateg

No man
Can be coaxed
From boyhood
During winter solstice.

Deep snows'
Long thighs
And mothers' soft songs
Induce sleep.

Soft blankets
Wrap themselves
Around the warmth
Of familiar sounds.

Soft flamelight
And family shadows
Thicken morning's depths
With favorite smells.

Long wood caches
Swollen pouches
Tight baskets
Fill men's senses like bellies full of fish.

Time to rest.

Mikchaawekwe

WOMEN'S WORK

He slips out
after every meal
with restlessness in his pocket.

She settles in
after every meal
with fatigue in her limbs.

He welcomes
long, low work sheds
with open doors that beg for sunlight.

He works
by lamplight
against stone and wood and precious metal.

She sorts through
great stores of pumpkins
looking for spoilage to whittle away.

She loves
to peel and carve
to dry and freeze and can.

He loves
to grease and polish
to drill and grind and form and create.

She lives
to maximize every moment
in favor of security and comfort.

He can taste
well-seasoned survival
in the months to come.

She can taste
sharp tools and competence
in the years to come.

She hears him
singing through his tools
rhythmically sawing, tapping, changing, maximizing
    resources.

She evaluates
need for consumption
among baskets and cold stores and jars.

He anticipates
tender sweets
and juicy meats.

He dances
out to his sheds
after every meal.

She dances
around her cook fire
before every meal.

Aandeg Bagoonsan

HOT TEA

Aandeg bagooooonsan . . .
>They say it like that, the sounds going through their
>noses,
>Like generations they've seen, but I have not.

Aandeg bagooooonsan . . .
>*That O, it goes up your nose, like in "fish."*
>Like everybody else in the world speaks
>>Anishinaabemowin (or should . . .).

Aandeg bagooooonsan . . .
>They are old and soft, sitting around that table, finally
>resting,
>Hugging the woodstove, shuffling cards, drinking hot
>tea.

Aandeg bagooooonsan . . .
>It means they're settled in now, anticipating one more
>winter,
>Assessing their stores; better save the peppermint for
>later.

Aandeg bagooooonsan . . .

> *Remember how you used to pick it like big bunches of*
> *flowers,* Noozhishen?
> Mine decomposing in a vase, a bouquet; yours hung
> from the ceiling.

Aandeg bagooooonsan . . .

> My husband does not understand why I snip it into my
> salad;
> Because that's how it went through my nose fresh in
> summer.

Aandeg bagooooonsan . . .

> *Remember how we used to make our own* zhiiwabo,
> Shiime?
> Like anybody outside that kitchen knew those salads.

Aandeg bagooooonsan . . .

> *Crow feathers!* Look, how the leaves change color, from
> bottom to top.
> A bunch of old scientists, explaining iridescence in
> ancient terminology.

Gaagaage bagooooonsan . . .

> Old men drifting through the kitchen, just to tease . . .
> *Add sugar,* wiisagaagamin i'iw naboob.

Gaagaage bagooooonsan . . .

Ombiigiziwag igiweg aandegwag gi kaagaagiwag
noondaagoziwaad.

*Those old crows and ravens make a lot of chatter when they
gossip.*

Manidoogiizis

SPIRIT MOON

When the fire is just right and the songs of his ancestors are
    tucked into the rafters just so,
When the scrapes of bowls and spoons and pots across
    wooden tables and benches melt into the softness of
    familiar voices and old, retold stories,
When dim light flickers and black spaces behind nothing
    push down on his awareness,

Spirits seep out of the floorboards like spring breezes and
    steam from fragrant teas.
Spirits take over the bodies and mouths and minds of the
    ones he loves.
Spirits tell their own stories in the worn clothing of his
    father's day in the woods, his grandmother's near-death
    illness, his mother's turnips peeled, his own conversation
    with a sun-loving snake.

Adikwag push open the doors, stumble about the tables,
    clacking together their antlers, spilling teas and nut
    bowls with their wide, wide buttocks, sniffing the air for
    remnants of their own flesh, singing of their own nutrient
    value.
Amikwag smack the woodstove with the flatness of their
    strong tails, resonating as lids upon stewpots.

Waabazhiishiwag blow pufflets of water gently from their
nostrils only inches from the boy's soft ear, then sleepily
wrap their long, downy bodies around his slim fingers and
toes.

Having been patient for long weeks, speared and racked,
filets-de-namegosag flee fireside heat to swim slowly in
thin smoke above the cupboards and a shelf that holds the
boy's stiff schoolbooks.
Adikamegwag frantically dance themselves into a powder
and fall into spinning soup bowls while uncles laugh and
wave their spoons.
From outdoors, namebinag laugh and tease that the ice is
still too weak to support mere human fishermen.

Old otter climbs up from under the porch and massages
Misho's sore knee, rubbing in rhythm to a song about
muscles and tendons and the urge to jump up out of bed
and dance.
Snapping Turtle lights his pipe with tinder, blinks to the
song beats, sings softly, like a rasp, sings of contentment.
Tree Frog climbs and leaps from one herb bundle to another,
shouting out the names of each, until everyone in the
room remembers, remembers, everyone remembers how
to heal.

Gegek wants more meat and more personal space, complains
that the party has gotten too big.

Ajijaak blows her nose loudly into her wing tips and more
loudly expresses her desire that more relatives fly in for the
party, in spite of deadly winds and drifting snows.

Maang scratches at the tabletop and insists that it is far
too late, far too resource consuming; it is time for some
of them to sleep and for some of them to go away, back
through the floorboards and the breezes at the frames of
windows.

When these things happen, lynx swim open waters to lend
an ear tuft to conversation.

Wolves hush one another and lick paws in yellow light cast
outside the windows of Ojibwe children.

Drowsy bears stir against closet doors like sleeping dogs in
the closeness of heat and food and family and comfort.

When soft blankets lay heavy and breathing against sounds
and songs and stories,

When steam and smoke and breath from a hundred, maybe
a thousand years, maybe forever, lift voices and memories,

When noise and quiet spin together with heat and chill and
fear and satisfaction,

It is said that even spruce grouse crouch under the wild roses
against the walls of that house, just to hear those stories.

Gaagkwe

PORCUPINE WOMAN

That name came to her
pretty early on,
'cause she didn't have a plan
when she woke up in the morning.

Her grandmother
used to say,
"A porcupine doesn't have a plan
when it wakes up in the morning."

She meandered
in the snow,
sang
when she made tracks.

She looped back on herself,
looking
for nothing in particular,
until she came home.

She never went far
from her house
or her grandmother
when she meandered.

It only made sense
that she would chase
after those porcupines
in the snow.

They looped back on themselves
not looking
for anything in particular,
maybe some green twigs.

Gaagobiwaian

PORCUPINE QUILLS

The first thing
she did
was thank
the animal

For giving
its life
to supplement
her income,

Although
she did not
think it fitting for Gaak
to supplement the entertainment of strangers.

So, she cooked
the porcupine
after she plucked it
from dawn to dusk

In a windless part
of the yard,
shooing away
pets and babies.

Her fingers
were raw
and stiff
from the cold.

Sometimes
the grease
from the animal's back
made her hands slip into the quills.

So, she wiped
the other hand clean
and grimaced
and pulled quills out of her own flesh

Without benefit
of a bullet to the skull
to stop
the pain.

She poked herself
when the children cried.
She poked herself
when she was tired.

She washed quills
and strained them,
plucking up strays
from the snow

Before she laid them out
to dry
like treasures
next to her woodstove.

She sorted quills
when she was too tired
to chase children
or chase porcupines.

She made pictures
of porcupines
on birch bark,
in tiny patterns of quillwork,

All the while
thanking the animal
for giving its life
to supplement her,

Although
she did not
think it fitting for Gaak
to supplement the entertainment of strangers.

She made baskets
with quillwork
by lamplight
as her children slept.

She poked herself
when the children cried.
She poked herself
when she was tired.

She lined up quills
between her lips,
like an extra hand,
let her work harder and faster.

She swallowed
invisible bristles
that made her throat ache
for days.

She poked her lips
when the children cried.
She poked her lips
when she was tired.

The first thing they did
when the children woke up
was admire
the delicate designs.

The first thing they did
when they woke up
was touch
the smooth patterns.

The first thing they did
when they woke up
was thank the animal
for supplementing their lives.

Miikagaagobiwaian

PORCUPINE QUILLWORK

People always asked her could she make some little quill boxes for them maybe real cheap.

Because times were tough and they didn't really need any quill boxes, but their grandmothers and their mothers had bought some quill boxes from some Indians a long time ago, and they were real cheap.

The Indians lived outside of the tourist town in a shack, hunting and fishing, and sometimes their family hired the man to do dirty work for them real cheap.

They used to buy firewood, too, from those Indians lived outside of town. Maybe five bucks; don't know how they could do it that cheap. Do you have any firewood we could buy from you real cheap?

That Indian lady, she used to make the baskets; she lined up those quills in her mouth, just like an extra hand, let her work faster. My mother bought those baskets from her real cheap.

Amazing how those Indians they could live on nothing like that, how they could make something out of nothing like that. We'd buy some of those baskets from you, too, if you've got some you could *sell real cheap.*

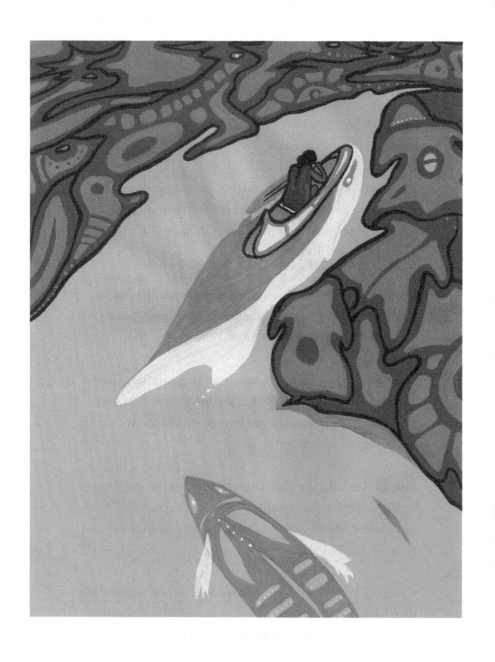

Namebinigiizis

SUCKER MOON

Shhh . . .
Put your head to the ice.

Shhh . . .
Pull the down and the cotton and the polyester and the thin-
   insulating special plastic fibers away from your ear.

Shhh . . .
Listen.

Shhh . . .
I want to talk to you about the sounds that the ice makes.

Shhh . . .
Do you hear the ice barking?

Shhh . . .
The ice is getting bigger, thicker.

Shhh . . .
This is good.

Shhh . . .
The ice is safe.

Shhh . . .
Listen to the place where the water drains into the lake.

Shhh . . .
Listen to the place where the water drains out of the lake.

Shhh . . .
Listen for namebiniig.

Shhh . . .
Listen, because the suckerfish know things you cannot
    know.

Shhh . . .
Suckers know the ice is getting thinner.

Shhh . . .
Listen for namebinag, breaking up sun-thinned ice.

Shhh . . .
Suckers need air.

Shhh . . .
Suckers break up sun-thinned ice.

Shhh . . .
Suckers know when lakes have gotten cold.

Shhh . . .
Suckers know when lakes stop making clouds.

Shhh . . .
Suckers know when sunshine thins ice.

Shhh . . .
Suckers know more than men about the change of seasons.

Shhh . . .
Suckers know about spring, even when it's far away.

Shhh . . .
Suckers know when to come upstream.

Shhh . . .
They've been doing this for thousands of years.

Shhh . . .
Just like me.

Shhh . . .
Put your ear to the ice.

Omashgewaading

LAKE ICE

They live in the biggest lakes, you know.
They know how to read water, temperature, sun.

They know when to break up river mouth ice,
For their upstream weddings and powwows.

Maybe you think they are ugly.
They have big lips on the bottoms of their faces.

Maybe you think they are ugly.
They do not readily anthropomorphize.

Maybe you think they are ugly.
They live on the bottom of your world.

You've heard they taste bad,
And they have too many bones.

But when the water is cold,
Their flesh is as sweet as their wisdom.

You've got to listen to them, you know.
They teach how to read water, temperature, sun.

When the biggest of the lakes have frozen over,
We can walk on water.

We have weddings and powwows,
Until schools of suckers tell us to stop.

You've got to listen.
I know you think there is no reason to listen to
  Anishinaabeg

Who claim to walk on water
Until ugly fish tell us to stop.

Niimik!

DANCE!

She'd been told
That there are Indians in exotic places
Who worship the solstices,
Scan the skies
For extremities tied by cosmic strings to the self-centered
  notions of longest and shortest.

She preferred
The less than exotic northern places,
Where solstices vanish under airborne moisture,
And Indians scan the skies
For the next day's weather forecast.

She'd been told
That during the shortest days of the year,
Lakes grow cooler,
And Indians scan the skies
For holes in the clouds, for lengthening days, for thick-safe
  lake ice, for familiar trails and shortcuts, for moonlit
  nights, for social events and family feuds and distant
  lovers . . .

She'd been told
That there are exotic places,
Where fish rise up from the bottoms of the lakes

And scan the skies,
For opportunities to dance across frozen waters like men
and wolves and moon-loving badgers and dry leaves in
cold winds.

She'd been told
That there are exotic places,
Where rabbits breed in leafless briars,
Scanning the horizons
For beautiful women with whom to share their warmth,
their softness, their scent, their skins, their very flesh.

She'd been told
That there are Indians in exotic places,
Who sip fragrant teas from sweet red rosehips,
Scan the skies
For the campfires of their ancestors on a northern horizon,
flickering to the rhythms of handheld drums and birch
bark rattles, deer toes tinkling like spring ice on a gentle,
warm beach.

She'd been told
That there are Indians in exotic places,
Who simmer long filets of savory meat and fish,
Scan the skies
For drum-wielding boys with protective bears in their
shadows, minnows and clams that sing from wavering
shorelines, and fish that dance between the stars.

Manidoominensag

BEADS

When the children are restless
     she spreads them out on the bedquilts
        like stars in a sky.

Children reach for colors
     touch coolness
        gather greedy piles of beauty and satisfaction.

Down through three
     back through two
Down through three
     back through two

Just like gichi-manidoo
     instructing our ancestors
        how to lay out patterns of scales on the fish.

Down through three
     back through two
Down through three
     back through two

Just like gichi-manidoo
    instructing our ancestors
        how to lay out patterns of hairs on the backs and
           chests of deer and moose.

Down through three
    back through two
Down through three
    back through two

Just like gichi-manidoo
    instructing our ancestors
        how to lay out patterns of waves sparkling across
           rivers and lakes.

Down through three
    back through two
Down through three
    back through two

Just like gichi-manidoo
    instructing our ancestors
        how to lay out patterns of clouds and stars across
           a black night sky.

Down through three
    back through two
Down through three
    back through two

Just like gichi-manidoo
        instructing our ancestors
                how to lay out patterns of children and
                        grandchildren against the swelling waves of
                        distant time and new generations.

Onaabinigiizis

CRUSTED SNOW MOON

Sometimes,
when my throat was sore
I would stay in the house
with the old lady
and she would make me drink
lukewarm teas made out of ozhaawajiibik
and I would say,
"This tastes like urine from the caribou,"
and she would say,
 "No, we use that for something else."

Kokomis Na

GRANDMOTHER

She could trick you into thinking
That a big muskeg fish with rows and rows of tiny teeth like
    sawblades
Would jump right up out of the nearest backbay and snatch
    you right up if you didn't-behave-in-this-little-boat-on-
    this-big-cold-lake-right-now.

She could lull you into thinking
That wild dogs yap after sunset, only because
They are fighting over the opportunity to creep in close to
    your sleeproom window to listen to the soft music of your
    breathing after you have fallen asleep.

She could coax you into thinking
That one more spoonful of soup, especially a couple more of
    those little skinny noodles out of a box
Would make the aching in your ears and the rasping in your
    throat and the tastelessness and the boredom go away.

She could frighten you into thinking
That if you didn't fill the woodbox with at least one more
    log,
Little People would creep across the crust of the snow and
    steal your favorite toys that you knew, you knew, just

where they were only yesterday when you were playing
with them under the bed.

She could lure you into thinking
That mashed pumpkin was your favorite food, again, even
    though
You would rather eat applesauce or sausages or potatoes or
    hot biscuits with ziinzibaakwad gi pamiida . . .

She could mislead you into thinking
That she could not chase you on icy, hard snow
If you mocked her and sang, "Kokomis na, kokomis na
    bidaasmiswe . . ."

She could fool you into thinking
That she could not chase you across a cold-morning lake
If you talked her into putting on ice skates and sang,
    "Chimiisningwe . . ."

She could remember you into thinking
That she could fly.

Ningizo

THAW

Shhh . . .
Put your ear to the ice
You can hear it.
It starts out slowly
Like the lazy stretching of winter-cramped limbs
By a mother bear on a sunny afternoon, after she has nursed
   her cubs.

Shhh . . .
Put your ear to the ice.
You can hear it.
It starts out gently
Like the lapping of wavelets
Encouraged by the drip drip drip of honeycombed ice.

Shhh . . .
Put your ear to the ice.
You can hear it.
It picks up momentum
Like the egotistical calls of courageous spring birds
   demanding space and spouse in exchange for a mere
   glimpse of showy, bright feathers.

Shhh . . .
Put your ear to the ice.
You can hear it.
It roars like mountainside cascades
Swollen and overcome with their own intensity, power, and
    progress.

Shhh . . .
Put your ear to the ice.
You can hear it.
It sings like thousands of voices
Circled around the same midwinter powwow blaze, sharing
    stories of past seasons, past ice packs, past jeopardy,
    past thaws, past renewals, past hopes, past hearts, past
    families, past cravings, past needs, past opportunities.

Bibookwedagaming

BROKEN

Sometimes I can't spend another minute with them.
There aren't enough comic books or card games or grilled
    cheese sandwiches
To make me keep loving them every minute of every day.
And I pray for winter's snows to become so heavy and wet
That they break the old leather bindings on ancient
    snowshoes.
That's how I know I can get away pretty soon, for invisible
    molecules of peace and quiet.

Sometimes I can't spend another minute with them.
There aren't enough songs or stories or traditions and love
To make me keep loving them back every minute of every
    day.
And I pray for late winter sun to heat the trunks of tall
    leafless trees
That will make sweet sap flow through our veins.
That's how I know that I can get away pretty soon, for some
    peace and quiet.

Ziinzibaakwadigiizis

MAPLE SUGAR MOON

Heh, heh, heh.
It's a sign
When the old man does that.

Heh, heh, heh.
He's laughing at himself
From maybe six or seven generations ago
Maybe a hundred
If you're lucky.

If you're lucky
You get to touch
A couple of those words
Come tumbling out of his mouth
Like ziinsibaakwadaboo
Where the birds have drilled a hole in the maple tree.

It comes out fast and thin
Like old men's words
Then thickens
When it gets to the bottom of the tree

Or the end of the story.
Then it's really sweet.

Nanaboozho gi Ziinzibaakwad

NANABOOZHO AND MAPLE SUGAR

He climbed up into the top of this tree.
The kids want to know why he climbed up into the top of this tree.

I don't know why he climbed up into the top of this tree, but maybe if you give me a little bit of time I can think up that part of the story, or maybe if you give me a lot time I can live that part of the story, but he climbed up into the top of this tree.

The kids want to know what kind of a tree.

Well, I can tell you what kind of a tree, because most of the time it's a maple sugar tree, although it doesn't really matter what kind of a tree, but I think the best kind of a tree is a maple sugar tree, so he climbed up into the top of this maple sugar tree.

The kids want to know if there is maple sugar in the maple sugar tree.

Well, yeah, there used to be all kinds of sugar in that maple sugar tree, but now there's not so much sugar in that maple sugar tree, and the Anishinaabe people, we've really got to work for that sugar up in the maple sugar tree, ever since he climbed up into the top of this maple sugar tree.

The kids want to know what happened to all the sugar in the maple sugar tree.

Well, that's what the story is about, how Nanaboozho made it so's there's not so much sugar up in that maple sugar tree, ever since he climbed up and he discovered all that sugar in the maple sugar tree, when he climbed up into that maple sugar tree, and he almost fell out of that maple sugar tree.

The kids want to know what Nanaboozho did when he climbed up into that maple sugar tree.

Well, you're just not making it very easy for me to tell you what happened to all the sugar up in that maple sugar tree, because it's all still there really, because all Nanaboozho did was make it harder to get all of the sugar out of the maple sugar tree, ever since he climbed up into that maple sugar tree.

The kids want to know why it's so hard to get all of the sugar out of the maple sugar tree.

That's what I'm trying to tell you. Nanaboozho poked his finger into the bark on the maple sugar tree.

The kids want to know why Nanaboozho poked his finger into the bark on the maple sugar tree.

I don't know why Nanaboozho poked his finger into the bark on the maple sugar tree, but maybe if you give me a little bit of time I can think up that part of the story, or maybe if you give me a lot time I can live that part of the story, but he climbed up into the top of this tree and he poked his finger into the bark on the maple sugar tree.

The kids want to know what happened next.

The sap came out very thick and sweet. It was *almost* sugar. Just a little bit of sunshine and it could have been sugar.

The kids want to know why it's not as thick and sweet anymore.

Nanaboozho just figured it might be too easy for his family that way, might be like trying to tell a story without any children around to draw it out and make it last for several days, to make me figure out the details, so you quit bugging me.

The kids want to know how kids draw out a story and make it last for several days.

Maybe you kids better go over to the other side of that big maple sugar tree there and make water. I'll be over here boiling the zhigiwin out of that sap.

Ziiinzibaaa Siigwankwad

SUUUGAAAR SPRING

There is nothing gentle
about the ruuush of water
and sustenance and strength
up the trunks and extremities
of sixty-foot-tall trees.

There is something urgent
about the instant flow
of clear sweet sap
from intrusive probes
by industrious animals and birds and men.

There is something soothing
about the tap, tap, tap of running sap
hurrying into a bucket
just for the gratification
of those who plan for future satisfaction in seasons to come.

There is something sensible
about the slosh of pails
spilled by tired men
and ambitious stumbling children
eager to give that first dipperful back to Mother Earth.

There is something cyclical
about the greed of the tree roots
taking back spilled pails
of their own lifeblood
while children wait in anticipation of the first maple sugar of
   the season.

Ziigwan

At the cusp of her own adolescence
when she herself was just beginning to bud
and grow upward and outward,
she was given the awesome task
of caring for her stubborn and forgetful grandfather

Who wandered about the village after dark,
often into the hours of dawn,
scattering handfuls of ice crystals and corn snow
across the landscape,
teasing lean foxes and bud-nibbling grouse.

His hair had grown long and wild,
streaked with yellow and dirt,
and he carried an old white blanket,
now heavy, damp, and gray—smelling of urine—
which he often snagged upon supple fruit canes

And threw frivolously over the gardens
of experienced farmers,
older women and men who knew
from years of experience and tolerance
the damage a loveable old man could do.

Sometimes they found him
with small piles of frozen songbirds
plucking away at their colored plumage
and roasting them on long sticks
grinning like a proud and hungry child.

So Ziigwan was given the burden
of wooing the old man back
into patterns of responsibility,
of wooing the old man back
into the rhythms of predictability.

He used to trick the child
into feeding swollen rosebuds to baby rabbits
from the palms of her smooth hands, smiling
while he danced behind her back
with big-bellied old women with names like Thundercloud

Who, like him, were forgetful
of seasonal changes and the fragility of new life,
while they jokingly set tip-up traps
of winnowing baskets full with fresh white snow
in treetops over workbenches and doorways.

He whipped up great bowls of wind
which he threw in Ziigwan's face
when she opened the door of his house
calling, "Grandfather, it's time to stretch and move,
time to clean house."

He showed his yellow teeth,
dragged his heavy, wet blanket all around the village,
threw chunks of ice at her from the roofs of houses,
called her insolent,
and in his confusion pushed her shoulders.
Her mother found her indoors, hiding
under rabbit-skin blankets, weeping,
so, she stroked the child's hair
and told her that only warriors hide under rabbit-skin
    blankets
in anticipation of great battles during snowstorms.

Her mother held Ziigwan's young body
close to her own large, soft form,
stroked her young cheek,
whispered that she now had other young ones to cuddle and
    nurture,
and told that girl to go outside,
"and
tell
that
old
man
to
STOP
playing
around
making
everybody
work

so

hard!"

So, Ziigwan took the old man's cool, frail hand
into her own warm hand, said softly,
"Grandfather, it's time to move to the north side of the
   village,
because you know how we depend
upon your strength and the gift of your watchfulness."

It was in this way
that Springtime walked northward,
wooed a tired and disoriented Winter into submission,
and grew into womanhood
among the blooms of wild red roses.

Waabigwanigiizis

FLOWERING MOON

Mornings
Light reaches long and low from the horizon
Like a child stretching for sugar
Touching glowing poplar blossoms
Like clusters of forgiveness for the harshness of winter.

Afternoons
Shadows reach long and low from the horizon
Flickering with the whims of wind and twig
Like flies humming in deep and out
Through maroon-striped throats of pulpit flowers.

Evenings
Moons rise over streambed willows
To ensure that silver cats' paws and yellowing catkins
Listen to beseeching tree frogs
That guide spiraling nighthawks through courtship and
    procreation.

Zhigaagawanzhiig

ONIONS

We used to dig up the wild leeks
And pull at dark green coils of wild garlic.
Our mothers would call us "stinky"
And throw us out of their kitchens,
Then poke their heads out their doors
And holler to bring back some of those later, for supper.

Bibiwazhashkwedoonsag

MUSHROOMS

As children
They swung like possums
On broken trees
Gifted to them
By winter winds

Tracked through winter-packed forest floors
Looking for uplifts and tufts among damp brown leaves

Crisp flowerheads
Sweet spotted lily leaves
Wrinkled mushrooms
Gifted to them
By recent snowmelts

As adolescents
They stole their mothers' paint pots
And colored hardwoods' understories
With Nanaboozhopikwanzh, multihued violets
Moccasin flowers and white men's breeches

Leaving youthful trails of pigment and disarray
With only a damp red brush to hurriedly finish off the
    trilliums

As lovers
They huddled like rabbits
Breathing in perfumes
Of their own contrivance
Under dallying tree buds

As patriarchs
They laughed like old crows
At armloads of dark forest mushrooms
Gifted to them
By children of the west wind.

Gichimikwamikwaamiknaakwag

ICE TURTLES

Shhh . . .
This is the chorus sung gently
Under exuberant screeching
At lakeside powwows
Where the smooth and the wet-skinned
Gather for ceremony and dance
Given the first opportunity
Of long, snow-free days
And open water on cold, still lakes.

Look . . .
From the gunwales of your canoe
Straight down a hundred feet or more
At underwater powwows
Where the smooth and the wet-skinned
Gather for ceremony and dance
Given the first opportunity
Of sun-warmed top waters
And slow-melt nutrients.

Feel . . .
The drip by drip stirring
Of great, sleeping ice turtles
At lakeside powwows
Where the smooth and the wet-skinned

Gather for dance and ceremony
Given the first opportunity
Of sun-warmed rocks and water-thrown light
In deep northern faces.

Sing . . .
Softly with cautious, ethereal turtles of ice
As they share safe-traveling songs
At lakeside powwows
Where the smooth and wet-skinned
Gather for dance and ceremony
Given the first opportunity
To slip cautiously, graciously
Into the warm, loving arms of the lake that birthed them.

Ode'iminigiizis

STRAWBERRY MOON

Years ago
a white woman tourist
gave her a picture
she had drawn
of the perfect Indian
and carefully instructed her
to look, act, and be
just like that make-believe Indian
and the white woman tourist
called her masterpiece
"Strawberry Moon"
but it did not in any way
lessen her love for strawberries
or picking them
in the sunshine
with loved ones
like young raccoons
and competitive crows
or late-nesting brown songbirds
that craved
the privacy of sunshine
among pink-fingered brown children
with berry-red lips.

Wigwaasimakakoon

BIRCH BARK BASKETS

Curiously, the individual who was chosen by the Great
Mystery to accurately share the secret of basketmaking with
Ojibwe women and girls

Was the offspring of an attractive young woman and the
west wind, was raised by a cantankerous grandmother, and
had a character as fickle as the circumstances of his birth.

So, he selected only the most discerning of Ojibwe women
and girls with whom to share this useful and artful
knowledge-gift.

And he wrapped his gift carefully in a bundle of long, hot
summer days tied up with basswood fibers using very
special, very difficult, tiny knots that even he could not
untangle.

It was only by virtue of her ingenious knack at disentangling
superfluous knots and her extremely good looks as well as
her reputation as a good cook and seamstress

That my grandmother was courted, actually stalked, at the
age of twelve or thirteen, by the instructive basket maker
himself.

It was with nimbleness of fingers and strong-armed foisting-
off of handsome and not-so-handsome men that my
grandmother practiced and honed to perfection her skill

At completely peeling the skin off of unsuspecting birch
trees on hot, summer afternoons, when she really should
have been taking her children or grandchildren for a
refreshing swim.

Confined by my own small stature and my status as a genetic
and mental receptacle for all things cultural, as well as my
ability and eagerness to paddle a canoe at a very young age

I was subjected to lengthy lessons on the proper means of
hunting the elusive perfect birch tree, as it crept, silently,
deeper and deeper into the woods, as far as possible from our
dormant canoe.

Upon our safe return—paddling into the wind for hours,
maybe days, on end—with a vessel-load of cool, wet bark,
appropriately weighted down with deadfall trees, antler
sheds, firewood, a couple of fresh trout, and maybe six or
seven rocks for some project she intended me to accomplish
in my free time,

Ninooko spread her goods out before her. Then she sang
sweet songs, peeled roots, snipped, stitched, punched,
sewed, folded, manipulated, realigned, configured,
reinforced, scraped, enhanced, and imbued with beauty

large stacks of winnowing baskets and storage packs for sugars and meats,

While I sat by quietly, in amazement, eating wild rice and sipping sweet tea.

Nimaamaa

MY MOTHER

At about the age of eight or nine
she watched as her mother silently slipped
off to the far side of the sweetgrass patch
to relieve herself, and
the child was disgusted by
the discovery of her mother's heavy-scented humanity.

Today she slips away
from her children and other responsibilities
to sit in that very same spot
just so that she can feel
like a little girl again.

And she cries in shame
then forgives herself
for her own humanity.

Aabita Niibin

SUMMER SOLSTICE

If you gave my father the opportunity
He would tell you
That during the summer
He worked twenty hours a day
And played for four.
But I know for a fact
That he enjoyed
Every minute of his life
Even when he was so tired
That he slept sitting up
In front of the fire
With me in his arms
While whitefish
Danced over the coals
On long greenwood planks
And our grandfathers
Had beach fires
In the skies over our heads
While whitefish
Danced over the coals
On long greenwood planks.

Miinikewigiizis

Sometimes in the morning
When only her children were asleep
Yet little birds and lizards sang
Sweet wake-up calls
Over the heads of dancing caribou
Trailed by a chorus line of fat merganser ducks
And a fireworks display of leaping minnows
Followed by falcons screeching, "Encore! Encore!"
And tall pine trees slapping their thighs in delight,
She snuck out back
Where a wild plum tree
Was flanked by the first sun-rich raspberries,
Black-ripe currants,
And the earliest tiny blueberries.
And in the shade of those fat plums
One found the last of spring's strawberries
Right next to the first thimbleberries
Above a sandy slope
Full with black, black dewberries
And just a handful of firm gooseberries,
Just past the spot
Where the blackcaps were winding down
From full production.

These things she would line up on the kitchen table
All in a row,
And then she'd sing good morning to her children
Repeating the few lines she could recall
From that particular morning's chorus line.

Gaagaagi Onagamon

SONG FOR A RAVEN

You   always seem to nest
Where I happen to be
In sun patches buried deep in the bush

So thick a man must duck and crawl and climb and loop back
    on himself
Just to be alone.

You   always seem to nest
Where I am most vulnerable
Picking sweetgrass in a windless hollow

With air just so thick from moisture and pressure to
    somehow perceive of myself as a dying breed.

You   always seem to nest
Where I hide when I feel most useless
In an upland moose meadow

Desperate for excuses to check on the success or failure
    of cranberry blooms no one of consequence is likely to
    harvest—except for waxwings and grouse and maybe even
    me and the songs I carry in my pocket for times like this.

You   always seem to nest
Where I come when I feel most exhausted
Hidden by mountains and forests and cold, deep lakes

Whose ragged no-trails are generation-built barriers to
    second-class citizenship and modern doubts of our
    competence, maybe even of our existence.

You   always seem to nest
Where I feel most powerful
On harsh peninsulas of wind

Dependent upon endangered resources taught to us by
    hungry, angry, underemployed Indian men and women
    half a lifetime ago . . . as they had been taught by others
    before them.

You   always seem to nest
Where I feel most protected
In nutrient-rich basins of survival

As your nervous wingbeats cast loud shadows, and your
    startling calls urge me to watch out, watch out, watch out
    for the Thunderbirds today.

You   always seem to nest
Where I feel most confident
On decaying, treeless cliff faces

Under your offspring-oriented eye with wide-angle lens and
   generations of mishaps, urging me to watch out, watch
   out, watch out for dangers less benign and helpful than
   electrically charged Thunderbirds.

You   always seem to nest
Where I seem most driven
Toward songs sung to wingbeats and nervous panting
   by Raven-Women-Mothers, builders of strong nests of
   watchfulness for reclusive offspring who never stop
   learning lessons for all of their lives . . . and maybe longer
   than that.

Nizhishenh

MY UNCLE

Even weeks
After
Summer solstice
The old man
Could still find
Patches of snow
In deep
Northern crevices
Where no sun
Ever ventured.

He would
Pack it home
To ice-down
Fish and meat
Whose availability
We
Took for granted.

Sometimes
My kids ask
How did he
Do that?
And I want
To take them out

To distant places
He took me
Because of that propane
They
Take for granted.

Sometimes
I want to
Strap them to my back
Like babies
And fly with them
To distant places
I used to take them
Where we
Would trick birds
Out of their first eggs

And bundle up
Steel-handled pails
Of survival
Just so that
They
Don't take
Me
For granted.

Ogaa-gitige

SHE GARDENED

My mother's garden
    was so big
        that raccoons and deer
            made offerings of tobacco
            at her feet.

She used to plant
    tall sunflowers and prickly pumpkins
    all around its perimeter
        to limit the extent
            of their indulgences.

My mother didn't let small children
    plant her garden
        so, we lay about its boundaries
            with a big brown dog
                and barked her love songs.

My mother didn't let anyone else
    inside her garden
        until the plants were big enough
            for clumsy children to step upon
            while she smiled.

My mother
        made something out of nothing
                in crooked rows
                        and scattered circles
                                where we grazed like lovers
                                        eager for the taste of forever.

Adikamekgiizis

WHITEFISH MOON

Before this place
Was as warm as it is today
We could count on the whitefish
To come into the shallows
With the dependability
Of thousands of generations
Of whitefish and eaters of whitefish.

My children remember this
In their own generation
And they are obliged to weep
For the thousands before them.

Gakaamikiijiwan

CASCADES

There is a place
Where two waterfalls come together
One warm
One cold
Like faucets
For those foolish enough
Or desperate enough
To climb up tall crevices
Behind boulders
Big enough
To hide
Long canoes.

The cascade is visible
Only in certain lights
From certain places on Lake Superior
And our ancestors
Used to have secret
Rendezvous
In this bath house
That the ancestors built
Just for Indians
Who needed to hide
From soldiers
And mercenaries

And black-robed priests
Indian agents
And baby thieves.

And we think of these things
Whenever
Summer's freedom
Seems to look short-lived
And squirming children feel
As ethereal as mist
That feeds upright ferns
On steep volcanic cliffs
Where two waterfalls come together
Just for Indians
Who need to hide
From treaties
And bendable laws
White teachers
And loss of identity
For those we love
And hide in crevices
Among the cascades
Of our best intentions
And sad, strong love.

Waanzhibiiyaaniing

POTHOLES

When we came back
From the path under red pines
That ran along certain sand spits
That separated pothole ponds
From the bigger lake

She would put on her glasses
Begin to cut out wormholes
And brown spots
From big, soft spongy-bottoms
That we brought her
From morning walks.

She would wave one arm
Over that way
Tell us that Anishinaabeg
Have always lived in this place.
You can tell
By what grows in those potholes

Fat ducks
And manoomin
Barely surviving
After the onslaught
Of lumbermen

Who crushed out life
With heavy loads of logs
Submerged
To keep out the sawyer bugs
That chewed away
At their future incomes
That they got for free
From simple Indians
Who failed to see
The proper use
Of a shallow pond.

Wiingashk
Mashkiigobag
Wiikenh
All recovering
From the ravages
Of progress
Under the straining eyes
Of Indian grannies
With stories for the future.

Ma'iingan Attikoon

A DAY OUT WITH MY DAUGHTER

She asked me how come they call it that, ma'iingan attikoon.

I told her that it's because the wolves roll around in it, when they find it. They flop around in it, when they find it. They flop down all happy and roll around with their tongues out . . . and all four feet up in the air waving around.

She asked me why they do that.

I told her that those soft white berries smash and get into their fur. Then they lie there in that ma'iingan attikoon, and they lick themselves.

She asked me why they lick themselves like that.

I told her that maybe they want to have minty fresh breath.

Manoominikegiizis

RICING MOON

An uncle on my father's side
laughed
when we brought home
handfuls of rice
from that small backbay pond,

Said he was gonna
show us how to do it right,
and the next year
came back to stay all summer
and tended that rice.

He pinched that rice,
he spoke to that rice,
he bundled it up just so,
and it would ripen the way
only an old man knew it could.

Then he took us out
in an old flat-bottomed boat
made us tap tap tap
those smooth cedar poles
made us tap tap tap.

Just an old man
Snorting
when the chaff went up his nose
rinsed his fingers in the lake
then took a drink.

He took us
through channels
over mudflat shallows
he'd contrived
with confidence.

We'd rise up on gunwales
rest on our hands
shift our weight
after the fat old guy
got his end stuck in shallow muck.

Every time we complained,
he'd have a story
that he told in detail,
burdening us with his memories
until we threatened to jump into the lake.

No more, no more, no more;
those old stories,
your faith,
are lost on summer hillsides.
But he said, "Not in shallow backbays."

Not on late summer days,
when self-centered boys
should learn
from old men
what praying is about.

We still had to parch the rice
we still had to husk the rice
we still had to winnow the rice
we still had to eat the rice
we still had to bless the rice.

We saw
a big snapping turtle,
big enough to nibble off
all of our toes,
but the old man just laughed.

I saw three big pike
close to the shore,
waiting patiently for minnows,
and I threw a handful of rice
but they were too smart.

I threw rice at the old man, sang out,
"Some for the ducks.
            For wooorms and snails and buuugs.
                    For the faaamily.
                            The rest for the bottom of the lake."

Abinibiikaa

WHEN THE WATER IS WARM

One summer
Some boys were diving from a cliff into Black River water
Just before the tannin hue dispersed into Lake Superior
And my mother took off her flowered black summer
    sundress
Right in front of those white boys
Because she knew she was beautiful.

Then she jumped right off that cliff with them.

And every year after that for the rest of my childhood
My father waded into the river, dove down in that very spot
To make sure that the Ice People had not moved any
    boulders during our absence.
Then we pulled off our clothing
And dove into the Black River in our underclothes
Because we knew we were beautiful.

Even dogs followed us over that cliff
Flew after us in clinging dependence and love
Barking with every leap and laughing with every leap
We took turns holding initiates in our arms
Until they were old enough to jump into a late summer river,
    too

Somewhere in respite between
Working for nothing and working for everything.
We were like fat fish looking for lovers
Before an autumn of harvest
Swelled our bellies and made us eager to sleep.

Ginozheg

PIKE

Every summer when lake trout hide down deep from
    summer's heat
Ninety horses plunge into the lake
With seven blind conservationists on their backs
Towing enough tents and gear
To conquer the Far North as efficiently
As they conquered the Wild West.

It is at my grandfather's old portage trail
Lined with medicine roots and soft thimbleberries
That they climb upon the shore
Guided by screams from spruce saplings underfoot
And greedily pull more than fifty fat pike
Out of the smallest inland lake,

Where even in my own recollection
Anishinaabe women in small canoes
Paddled by young hungry children
Could depend upon the late summer kindness of Ginozhe
When the men from our village were forced away to jobs in
    steel mills
By strangers on the backs of Evinrude stallions
And even the lake trout hid deep from late summer's heat
Out of our reach.

Mishi Ginebigook,
Animikiig Dash

Underwater giants, Thunderbirds, too.

Our parents   are ancestors.

Our grandparents   are strong trees in the forests.

Our stories   are textbooks.

The lakes   are libraries.

We are told that Cougars live underwater,
Their tails great, muscular swells
Manifesting themselves as memories of yesterday's winds,
Pushing us from open lake to crushing shores.

We are told that Thunderbirds sweep out from the lakes,
Their wings pushing new winds into chops
Manifesting themselves as reminders that everything
    changes,
Pushing us from small, safe bays to the uncertainty of open
    water.

We slide through life in the empty spaces,
Between muscular swells and abrasive, short waves
Pushing in opposition to one another,
Manifesting ourselves as survival, adaptation, Anishinaabe
    hopes.

Underwater giants, Thunderbirds, too.

Our clans   are universities.

Our families   are waves of moving molecules.

Our lives   are starlight.

We   are the sun and the moons.

We are told that Great Antlered Snakes live in river mouths,
Their attitudes and whims huge, muscular swells
Manifesting themselves as socioeconomic forces,
Pushing and pulling us between safety and insecurity.

Underwater giants. Thunderbirds, too.

Our traditions   are maps.

Our language   is history.

Our tomorrows   are great basins.

Our stories   are real.

Mishi Ginebigook, Animikiig dash.

ACKNOWLEDGMENTS

"Miinikewigiizis: Blueberry Picking Moon" was published in *Goose Journal*, Spring 2022.

"Bagaanag: Plenty" and "Aandeg Bagoosan: Hot Tea" were published in *Navigations: A Place for Peace, About Place Journal*, Spring 2022.

"Onaabinigiizis," "Gaagobiwaian," "Gabo Wendaamowin," "Waawaashkeshikwe," and "Aandeg Bagoonsan: Hot Tea" were published in *Hanging Loose 112*, Spring 2022.

"Gabo Wendaamowin" was also published in *Navigations: A Place for Peace, About Place Journal*, Spring 2022.

"Manidoogiizans: December" was published in *Sing: Poetry from the Indigenous Americas*, edited by Allison Hedge Coke, published by The University of Arizona Press, 2010, and in *Split This Rock Journal*, March 2015.

GLOSSARY OF OJIBWE TERMS

Note: Languages reflect cultural concepts that can't always be translated word for word. Since Anishinaabe families and social groups have varying slang terms for ideas and words, and sometimes this slang has been influenced by European languages that we also speak, this glossary should not be used as a definitive source for translating ideas between English and Anishinaabemowin (Ojibwe/Chippewa). I've taken liberties with sound, imagery, and meaning in both languages. Anishinaabe pronunciation and subsequent English spelling of Anishinaabe words also change depending upon the sounds preceding a word in a sentence, so there is no way to accurately spell or define them when interjecting them into a text that combines languages.

Aabita niibin: The middle of the growing season, when trees are leafed out; solstice.

aandeg bagoonsan: "Crow feather-leaves," a leafy plant eaten fresh in summer and dried for winter.

aandegwag: Crows.

abinibiikaa: Summertime, when the water is warm.

achiiside: Abdominal cramps.

Adikamekgiizis: Whitefish Moon.

adikwag: Caribou (plural).

adikamegwag: Whitefish (plural); literally caribou from the lake or underwater caribou—a reference to how they school in large numbers and to their traditional use as a readily available source of protein.

ajiijak: Crane, a symbol of leadership.

amikwag: Beavers, symbols of industriousness.

animikiig: Thunderbirds, giant eagles who live in the clouds and whip up fresh winds by beating their wings. They shoot thunderbolts out of their eyes, especially when they are upset. Stories about their constant battles with lake-dwelling characters, such as *Mishi Bizhiiw*, the Underwater Mountain Lion, are a mnemonic device for teaching young people living around the Great Lakes about old swells under the surface of the water versus new chop on top of the water and how to manage a water-craft in shifting winds.

Anishinaabeg: "Original people," the name we use for ourselves.

Anishinaabemowin: This is the name we use for the language spoken by many tribes for several thousand miles/kilometers of territory surrounding the Great Lakes. There are sub-languages, or dialects, that merge into one another, changing from one neighboring community to another.

bagaanag: Hazelnuts; also implies competence or industriousness; can be used in rare contexts as slang for greed, because hazelnuts are rich and fatty, and can suggest a lack of clarity because husking hazelnuts dyes the fingers black.

bagoonsan: A kind of mint.

bibiwazhashkwedoonsag: A kind of mushroom; wrinkly fungus.

Bibookwedagaming: Broken snowshoe season; can refer to late winter/early spring, when ground snow becomes mushy and heavy.

Biboon: Literally, all growth stops here, now. A personification of the season of winter arriving as a young man and transforming into a stubborn elder as the season progresses. He has the responsibility of providing plant life with the opportunity to rest, but he frequently overstays his welcome.

bidaasmisswe: Something is making a beeline toward you.

chimiisingwe: Hair on face; monster; scary person; epithet used by children.

dash: And, too, also.

dibikateg: Darkness.

gaagaagi onagamon: Ravens' song; implies persistence and longing.

Gaagkwe: Porcupine Woman; persistent woman.

gaak: Porcupine.

gaagaage: Raven.

gaagobiwaian: Porcupine quills.

gabo wendaamowin: Smothered feeling, sense of being overwhelmed.

Gashkadinogiizis: Ice-Forming Moon.

gakaamikiijiwan: Waterfalls, cascades.

gi: And.

Gichi-manido: Great mystery; a creator.

gichimikwamikwaamikinaakwag: Large ice formations
lingering on north-facing crevices on the shore of Lake
Superior in early summer; they predictably melt into the
shapes of various animals in a sequential manner. They
symbolize the water cycle of evaporation and precipita-
tion, repetition, and predictability.

gegek: Sparrow hawk.

Gidanimibiisaa na: Let's paddle away; I'm taking you with
me.

ginebigoog: Snakes; also frothing rapids in waterways, cur-
rents, sine-generated curves, fish-tail movement, objects
in tow.

ginozhe: Pike; long and skinny.

igiweg: Those things over there (that are alive).

innizhisheenh: My uncle (on my mother's side).

iwe: That.

kokomis na: Our grandmother.

Kokomis na bidassmiswe: Here comes Grandma! (a line from a comical children's song).

maang: Loon; a symbol of leadership.

ma'iingan attikoon: Snowberries.

Manidoogiizans: Little Spirit Moon, usually December because it is the moon of winter solstice, of Christmas.

Manidoogiizis: Spirit Moon; Mystery Moon, usually January because it follows solstice.

manidoominensag: Literally "spirit berries"; glass beads obtained through trade, incorporated into Anishinaabe culture and used to continue producing traditional designs that were originally made with porcupine quills and caribou or moose fur.

manisaanabe: Play on words—one who provides firewood.

manoomin: Wild rice; literally, "good berry." This is a high-protein wild grass seed that traditionally is harvested and traded in vast quantities at the end of summer. It's also used to attract waterfowl and other forms of wildlife. Anishinaabe people today are protecting and revitalizing this form of agriculture.

Manoominikegiizis: Ricing Moon.

mashkiigobag: A wetland-growing heather harvested for tea.

mishi ginebigook: Literally, they are big snakes; some snakes, of various sizes and personalities, were given the gift of antlers by their creator. They inhabit all bodies of water, including springs, streams, seeps, and ponds. Sometimes they battle with Thunderbirds. Mostly they trip creatures with big feet, like people and moose. They look a lot like driftwood.

miikagaagobiwaian: Quillwork; designs made with porcupine quills softened and inserted into leather or birch bark, used to decorate storage containers and traditional clothing. This art form is still practiced by the Anishinaabeg.

mikchaawekwe: Work traditionally done by women; something made by a woman.

miigaadi: Strain against something

Miinikewigiizis: Blueberry Picking Moon.

minaniki: Pick berries.

minowichige: Being responsible.

mingiiskodee: Spring thaw.

Misho: Grandfather.

naboob: Soup (in this case, making fun of a bitter tea).

Namebinigiizis: Sucker Moon; the time in early spring when fish begin to swim upriver to spawn.

namegosag: Lake trout, deep-water trout (plural).

Nanaboozho: Also called Nanabush, Manaboozhoo, or Wanaboozho; an ancestor/relative/hero of the Anishinaabe people who is known for being creative but also makes mistakes. He is a son of the west wind but is half human and highlights our weaknesses and challenges.

Nanaboozhopikwanzh: A spring wildflower used for bug bites; refers to a comical traditional story.

namebinag: Suckers; bony, bottom-dwelling fish with sweet flesh, obtained when they come up river mouths in the spring. They often appear in such large numbers that they break up thinning lake ice with their sheer mass.

niimik: Dance!

nimaamaa: My mom.

ningizo: Thaw.

Ninooko: My grandmother, Grandma.

Noko: Grandma.

noondaagoziwaad: Generate a ruckus.

Noozhishen: Granddaughter.

Ode'iminigiizis: Strawberry Moon.

Ogaa-gitige: She gardened.

omashgewaading: Freezing, solidifying; a reference to a traditional song about reliance upon gifts brought by the North Wind.

Onaabinigiizis: Crusted Snow Moon.

ozhaawajiibik: Yellow root; goldenthread, a kind of medicine gathered near water seeps.

pagaask waashkaa: Waves hitting against rocks.

papashkikiu: Tea made from balsam growth buds.

shiibshiibshiib: Sound made by merganser ducks.

Shiime: A term used when addressing a younger sister; a small bird that stays close by.

waabazhiishiwag: Pine marten, a kind of weasel trapped for clothing and food; symbolizes fearlessness and dedication.

Waabigwanigiizis: Flowering Moon.

Waatebagaagiizis: Changing Color Moon.

wapooswawaaskwanminan: Slang for rose hips (bunny berries), derived from a story; also called *aginiimin*, prickly berry.

waanzhibiiyaaniing: Ponds, potholes, small basins feeding larger lakes.

Waawaashkeshikwe: Deer Woman; any girl or woman belonging to a clan represented by an animal with antlers; a woman who works hard to provide.

wigwaasimakakoon: Baskets made of birch bark.

wiikenh: A summer-flowering plant used for medicine.

wiingashk: Sweetgrass, a fragrant basket-making material; sacred plant of the north.

wiisagaagamin: Something tastes bitter.

zhigaagawanzhiig: Onions, smelly bulbs, stinky stuff; also, a bad pitch in baseball.

zhigiwin: Fluid, often urine.

Ziigwan: Personification of the spring season; an adolescent girl given the responsibility of urging Biboon (Winter) to return to his home in the north; an inexperienced young adult; freshening, improvement, growth, change.

zhiiwabo: Vinegar made from sweet mountain ash tree sap.

ziinzibaakwad gi pamida: Maple sugar and butter.

ziinzibaakwadaboo: Maple tree sap.

Ziinzibaakwadigiizis: Maple Sugar Moon.

ABOUT THE AUTHOR

LOIS BEARDSLEE is an Anishinaabe author, illustrator, and poet from Michigan's northern Lower Peninsula. Her works have received several nominations and awards, and in 2021 she was the first Native American author to receive Michigan's Notable Book Award for *Words like Thunder: New and Used Anishinaabe Prayers* (Wayne State University Press). Her writing has been featured by numerous journals and publications, such as *New York Times Magazine*, *Terrain.org*, *Yellow Medicine Review*, and Michigan Public Radio. Her artwork is currently a part of the collection at the Detroit Institute of Arts.